THE REAL THING

A Skill-Building
Book and Video
that Prepares
Students for
College Success

Martha E. Kendall

ISBN 0-945783-05-1

cover design by Alice McKown

"Borders" by Pat Mora used by permission of
Arte Publico Press
University of Houston
Houston, TX 77204-2090

Highland Publishing
P. O. Box 554
Los Gatos, CA 95031-0554
U.S.A.
fax (408) 353-3388
phone (408) 353-5756
esl@highlandpublishing.com

Table of Contents

Preface

The Real Thing prepares students to enter the mainstream curriculum at an American college. The video contains fifteen authentic college classes, each ten to fifteen minutes long. The skill-building book teaches students how to learn from them.

The professors on the video have taught in a wide variety of disciplines at colleges and universities across America. These lectures contain typical examples of topics they cover in introductory courses. Viewers observe what is expected in a college classroom; they see how teachers and students interact within a range of lecture and discussion styles, and they listen to spontaneous classroom language.

Pre-listening activities in the book prepare students for the videotaped classes. During the first three lectures, students are guided in their listening, focusing on information needed to answer comprehension questions. In the fourth unit students analyze an example of notes. In subsequent units, students take their own notes.

Every unit directs students in responding to the lecture: what to do with the information and how to predict what the professor expects them to know. The progression of topics moves from general college orientation to more demanding material. The book's early units focus on vocabulary development, basic notetaking, study skills and summarizing. Students practice critical thinking skills in later units, developing their intellectual aggressiveness; they learn to question, apply concepts and synthesize ideas.

To help students succeed in courses packed with large amounts of objective information, the book gives strategies for memorizing. Preparing for quizzes and essay exams is emphasized throughout, and every unit concludes with writing topics that relate to the lecture. Many oral activities for small groups prompt students to listen attentively to each other, because the individuals and groups are accountable for completing their tasks. In group interaction students develop cooperative social skills needed in many academic and professional settings.

The Real Thing makes a much-needed bridge for students in advanced courses of English as a Second Language as they prepare to move from a classroom in which they listen to comprehend to an academic classroom in which they must listen to learn.

Other students can also benefit from *The Real Thing*. Throughout the curriculum, motivated students may do poorly because of their anxiety about speaking in front of others, their reluctance to ask questions or express original opinions. Some bright students fail because they lack effective study skills. Practicing with *The Real Thing* helps them develop their potential.

The Real Thing can be used anywhere; it does not presuppose residence in the United States. It is appropriate in an advanced course in English as a Second Language, a College Orientation Program, a General Study Skills class or an individualized lab. (Lab users disregard each unit's section called "Discuss.") An Answer Key is available, suitable for reproduction at the instructor's discretion.

Depending on the needs of the students, instructors may choose to show a videotaped lecture once for general comprehension, and then replay it, stopping it every few minutes to ask students to summarize what was said, predict what will come next, check their notes for accuracy, respond to questions from the book, or to ask their own questions.

I owe thanks to more people than I can possibly list here for their help and suggestions during the creation of *The Real Thing*; however, I particularly want to acknowledge the support of Marsha Chan, Ray Collins, Jennifer Costanza, Denise Douglas, Lora Glaser, Lois Janowski, Karen Mann, Carole Mawson, Margaret Muench, Novella Simonson and Carol Wilson. My biggest debt of gratitude is to my husband, Joe Weed, for his technical, logistical and emotional support; and to our children, Jeff and Katie, for their love, generosity and inspiration.

Martha Kendall
San Jose City College

Please forward your comments about *The Real Thing* to: Executive Editor, Highland Publishing, P. O. Box 554, Los Gatos, CA 95031-0554, U.S.A.

Unit 1

Skills for College Success
a Counseling Lecture
by
Bill Bronson

I. Before the Lecture

The vocabulary used at a college is quite specialized. To help you understand this lecture, review the vocabulary below.

community college: a two-year institution of higher learning that awards A.A. (Associate of Arts) and A.S. (Associate of Science) degrees. ("Two-year" means that full-time students can earn their degrees in two academic years; however, many students attend part-time and take more than two years to earn a degree.) Students are called freshmen and sophomores, and the course work is "lower division."

college: a four-year institution of higher learning that awards B.A. (Bachelor of Arts) and B.S. (Bachelor of Science) degrees. ("Four-year" means that full-time students can earn their degrees in four academic years; however, many students attend part-time and take more than four years to earn a degree.)

university: an institution of higher learning that awards B.A. and B.S. degrees as well as graduate degrees such as an M.A. (Master of Arts) and M.S. (Master of Science) and possibly the Ph.D. (Doctor of Philosophy) and advanced degrees in medicine, dentistry and law.

college graduate: a person with a B.A. or B.S. degree is commonly referred to as a college graduate or college "grad," regardless of whether the degree was earned at a college or university. In conversation, "college" and "university" are often used interchangeably.

to drop a class: to discontinue or withdraw from a course, receiving no grade or units of credit for it

to add a class: to enroll in a course after regular registration has ended

Incomplete: a grade indicating that due to circumstances beyond the student's control, required work in a course was not finished within the course's time limits. However, when the work is done, a grade will be given, and the student will receive units of credit for the course. If the work is not finished, the Incomplete grade converts to an *F* or *No credit* grade.

F or **No credit**: The student's transcript (report card) will show that the student did not complete the work required to gain units of credit for a particular course.

Grade Point Average: The "G.P.A." is the cumulative average of a student's grades received for every semester in college. Most colleges assign grades on a 4-point scale:

$$4 = A \text{ (excellent)}$$
$$3 = B \text{ (good)}$$
$$2 = C \text{ (satisfactory)}$$
$$1 = D \text{ (unsatisfactory)}$$

prerequisite ("pre" means "before," and "requi" means "required"): a course that students must take before they are eligible to enroll in the next, higher level one

semester vs. **quarter**: Most colleges organize an academic "year" from September until June into two semesters; a short optional summer semester is also offered. A full-time student on the semester system enrolls in at least twelve, and usually fifteen, units per semester in the academic year. Most courses are for three units; the student attends each class for three hours weekly.

Some colleges divide the calendar year into four quarters – three during the traditional academic year, and the fourth during the summer.

to transfer: to change from one college to another. A student must request that units of credit for courses already taken will be granted by the new college. Courses usually are considered "transferable" if the material covered in them is equivalent (the same) at both colleges.

II. Comprehend the Lecture

As you watch the lecture, answer the following questions. Whenever you need more time, stop the tape. Rewind it if you want to hear a section again. Listen to the lecture as many times as you wish.

1. What is the first level of higher education?

_____

2. What degrees can be earned at this level?

_____

3. This level is sometimes called a_____ - year institution.

4. The second level is sometimes called a _____- year college.

5. What degrees can be earned at this level? _____

_____

6. What is the third level?_____

7. What additional degrees can be earned at this level?

_____

8. (yes, no) Will the instructor of a course automatically drop you if

you stop attending? _____

9. What is the only dumb question?_____

_____

10. List three things you should know about your professors:

_____

11. How many times do most college students change their majors?

_____

12. What are the two types of requirements students must fulfill?

_____

13. Why might it be a good idea to take G.E. classes first?

_____

14. What is an educational plan?_____

_____

15. Mr. Bronson says, "It's not anyone's job to tell you; it's your job to

_____."

16. List three typical forms used by students to make changes:

_____

17. To prepare for most careers, is it better to specialize or to train in a

variety of areas?_____

18. Name at least two services most colleges offer their students:

_____

19. (yes, no) Are lower division courses at a community college usually

equivalent to courses at a four-year institution?_____

20. Give at least one advantage of a community college over a four-

year institution:_____

III. Respond to the Lecture

The lecturer emphasizes that you should ask questions. How are you supposed to do this?

1. Learn the names of your professors. Most prefer to be addressed by title and last name: for example, "Mr. Bronson" or "Ms. Wolfe" ("Ms." is the general title for professional women, comparable to "Mr." for men.) If your professor has a Ph.D. (Doctor of Philosophy) degree, call him or her "Doctor," as in "Dr. Gutierrez." If you do not know whether your teacher has a Ph.D., you may use the general title, "Professor," as in "Professor Collins."

Many colleges and universities use titles to indicate the rank of faculty members, distinguishing between "Lecturer," "Instructor," "Assistant Professor," "Associate Professor" and "Full Professor." However, in general usage most Americans refer to college teachers as "professors " or "instructors," and a "lecturer" is anyone who gives a lecture.

2. Ask your professor where his/her office is, and his/her hours. Most professors spend several hours every week in their offices to be available to answer students' questions. It is particularly important to see the professor if you are having difficulty in a course. S/he may be able to help you directly, or refer you to someone who can. The professor wants you to succeed, but it is your responsibility to take the first step if you need help.

3. Take advantage of services, people and information sources on campus, such as counselors, librarians, the health center, tutoring, career and placement offices, and financial aid offices.

IV. Summarize

Use each lecture in *The Real Thing* as an opportunity to practice summarizing. You will need to recognize and list the lecturer's key points, put them into your own words, and then write them in well-connected sentences. Here is a summary of Bill Bronson's lecture. After each of the other lectures, write your own.

Summary of
'Skills for College Success'
a lecture by Bill Bronson

The first level of higher education is the community college, a two-year institution that offers an Associate of Arts (A.A.) or Associate of Science (A.S.) degree. A four-year college gives a Bachelor of Arts or Science degree. A University gives a Bachelor's as well as a Master's and possibly a Doctor of Philosophy degree, too.

If you want to drop a class, do not just stop attending it, because the professor doesn't automatically drop people who don't show up. There are forms for dropping a class.

The only dumb question is one you don't ask. Find out your professors' names, office locations and hours.

Many students change their majors, so it's smart to take general education requirements first, and major courses later on. See a counselor and make an educational plan so you know what courses to take for the degree you want. It's better to take courses in a lot of general areas, and a minor that's quite different from your major, so that you are prepared for more than one career.

Colleges offer many services; you just have to ask questions to find out about them.

V. Discuss

1. Many successful students study in groups, compare notes with other students, and become active participants within a community of learners. In order to feel more comfortable with your classmates, get to know them. First, form pairs. Then, interview your partner, asking for such information as hometown, major, employment experience, family situation, favorite hobbies, and anything else you think is relevant and you have time to find out about. After the interviews, introduce your partner to the class as a whole.

2. In groups of three to five students each, compose definitions of an ideal student. Choose a recorder to write your group's definition down in a few sentences. Then, choose a speaker to read your group's definition aloud to the class. Do the definitions composed by the different groups have any elements in common? How close do YOU come to being an ideal student?

3. Make a journal or log. Have class members suggest headings that identify general, daily activities of students. Using those that are appropriate for your life style, design a journal for keeping track of how you spend your time. Then, every day for a week, fill out your journal. How do you spend your time? Is this the way you think you should be spending your time?

4. Explain to a partner what major and career you are considering and why. Then your partner will summarize what you've said for the class as a whole.

5. If you are at a college, have each student research one service offered on your campus and report to the class what you've learned. For example, find out about the health service, tutoring, library, child care facilities, financial aid, scholarships, job placement, etc. Bring to class any forms needed to apply for such services and explain how they should be filled out.

   If you are not at a college, see if your library has any American college catalogs. Have each student get specific pieces of information about the colleges. Perhaps your counselor or teacher can acquire a college application form. Make multiple copies and try filling it out.

6. With a partner, role play a visit to a professor during his/her office hours. Plan what you want to ask, such as where you can get help in writing a paper or in comprehending the reading assignments. Let other students watch and make suggestions.

VI. Write

1. Topics one through five in *V. Discuss* can be developed as papers.

2. In what way(s) do you hope to benefit from your college education? Answer as fully as you can.

3. Write a paper describing a teacher who has had a particularly strong influence on you and why.

4. What was the most important question you have ever asked? Explain the question and its consequences.

5. What was the most important question you did not ask? Explain the situation and its consequences.

6. On its application for admission, an elite university asks applicants to respond to one of the following topics. Write an answer to whichever one you choose:

   • If you were to write a book, on what theme or subject matter would it be based, and why?

   • Tell us about one of the best conversations you've ever had.

Unit 2

Expectations of a College Student
a Counseling Lecture
by
Suzanne Gutierrez

I. When the Lecture Begins

A. Be in the right place at the right time. "The right time" is a few minutes early so that you can find a good seat – a place where you can see the blackboard and hear the professor well.

B. Bring necessary supplies. These include a pen or pencil and notebook (spiral or 3-ring binder) or a computer. Also, bring the textbooks. Label everything with your name and phone number.

C. Read the assignment in advance, and review it before class begins. Your textbooks reflect your conscientiousness. Respond actively to the content of your books, and write comments in them that make the books your own. Think of reading as your conversation with the text.

Often the best-loved books are those that have been read and thought about the most – and marked up the most. How do you read a book actively? If you are assigned to read a chapter from your textbook, follow these steps:

1. Begin by skimming the entire chapter. Get a sense of what is covered. Each part of the chapter will be easier to understand when you know how it fits in the whole.

2. Write down your own questions about the chapter. Then, when you read, look for answers to your questions. Questions may come from headings in the chapter. For example, if an italicized heading says "Attendance Is Important," ask: "Why is attendance

important?"

3. Underline or highlight topic sentences, definitions, summary statements and information that answers your questions. Do not underline everything. As you decide whether information is worth underlining, you are simultaneously reacting to it and well on your way to learning it.

4. Make notes in the margin of your book. For example, the notes might be:

- a key or star – an important concept you should understand
- a question mark – something you will need to ask the teacher to explain
- a reminder to check a word in the dictionary
- a reminder to compare this information with something else
- numbers identifying related ideas
- a summary of a major concept
- an arrow between similar or contrasting ideas
- your own symbols

5. Review the chapter, answering your questions.

6. If the chapter concludes with a summary or study questions, look them over carefully. They show what the author thinks is most important.

7. Try to predict what questions your professor might ask about the chapter. Plan your answers to those questions.

II. Comprehend the Lecture

Listen attentively to the lecture and answer the following questions. Whenever you need more time, stop the tape. Rewind it if you want to hear a section again. Listen to the lecture as many times as you wish.

1. List the five points Dr. Gutierrez says she will discuss:

_____

_____

2. *Success* may mean something different to each person. What

example does a student give of *success*? _____

_____

3. *Strength* may mean many different things. In terms of college,
    what does Dr. Gutierrez mean by "strength"?

_____

4. Name two ways a student can overcome problems in a course:

_____

_____

5. Give an example of something about which a counselor might
    provide advisement to a student:

_____

6. Give an example of a service that a career center might offer:

_____

7. What is the most important thing a student should do?

_____

8. What might happen if a student misses the first day or week of

class? _____

9. (yes, no) Will attendance affect your grade?_____

10. (yes, no) Is it considered rude for a student to ask the instructor a

question during a lecture? _____

11. (yes, no) If you have a question about the lecture, is it considered

polite to ask the instructor about it outside of class? _____

12. What three main responsibilities does Dr. Gutierrez say students

have?_____

_____

_____

13. What does *plagiarism* mean? _____

_____

14. What can be the consequences of *plagiarism*? _____

_____

15. In what way can students demonstrate responsibility and personal

discipline?_____

_____

III. Anticipate What You Will Be Expected to Know

1. The lecturer has written on the board the five points she plans to

discuss. On a quiz, she might list those five points and ask students to explain the meaning and significance of each. To prepare for such a quiz, look at the list of points covered in the lecture. Then look away from your notebook, and try to explain what each point means. If you can't think of much to say, review your answers to the questions in *II. Comprehend the Lecture.*

2. Be sure to attend the class right before a quiz or exam. Listen carefully for clues that the instructor may give about what to study. For example, the instructor might say, "This is important," or "I want to emphasize..." or "Be sure to go over...."

3. Ask yourself what kinds of quizzes and tests the instructor has given before. Learn from past experience.

4. Develop your own opinion about the material. What do *you* think about the ideas? Relate the lecture information to your life or your reading. It is common for a quiz or exam to ask you to provide your own examples of an idea or principle explained in class – not the examples given by the professor.

5. Compare the ideas with those in your text or in the preceding lecture.

6. For every course, create your own vocabulary list, and study new words. You can assume that if the lecturer takes the time to define a word, then she considers it important.

To be sure you know the meanings of terms Dr. Gutierrez uses, write their meaning and a specific example of each:

1. *advisement*

definition:_____

example:_____

2. *student conduct*

definition:_____

example:_____

3. *plagiarism*

definition:_____

example:_____

IV. Summarize

Write a summary of this lecture. It should be about ten to twelve sentences long. Use your own words, paraphrasing what the lecturer has said.

V. Discuss

1. Have all the students (and perhaps the teacher as well) write on a small piece of paper a word or phrase that explains what *success* means to them. Do not use names. Collect the papers, and have volunteers read the definitions aloud. Discuss differences and similarities. After hearing others' opinions, do any students want to change their definitions?

2. On a slip of paper, have each student write one thing that a counselor can do to help a student succeed in college. Collect the slips, and have volunteers read them aloud. Write the suggestions on the board, and then rank them in order of importance.

3. In small groups, make two lists: one of "Do's" and one of "Don't's" for new college students unsure about their responsibilities. Write your lists on the board. Have the class as a whole select the seven most important ideas. Write them in your own notebook.

4. If you are at an American college, have each person in your class interview two students who have been enrolled in the general college curriculum for at least one year. The purpose of the interview is for

the experienced students to explain to you what they think are the most important things a student needs to know in order to succeed. Plan your questions in advance, and summarize for your classmates your interviewee's advice. Conclude your summary with your opinion.

5. Research the job outlook for a career you're interested in. If your class is large, divide it up into small groups of people interested in similar careers. Exchange information. If your class is small, each student can report to the whole class what s/he's learned. Include this information for each career:

- required education or training
- availability of positions now
- job outlook in five years
- starting wages or salary
- opportunity for advancement
- why this career interests you

6. Without using names, have each student write on a piece of paper one possible quiz question based on Dr. Gutierrez's lecture. Exchange the questions, have each student read the question aloud that s/he received, and then explain the answer to it.

VI. Write

1. The topics in *V. Discuss* can be developed in writing.

2. If you are familiar with expectations of college students in another country or culture, contrast them with expectations of students in the United States.

3. Contrast the expectations of high school students with those of college students.

4. Imagine that you have been asked to write the introduction to a new textbook. The author wants you to explain to students how they can

get the most out of the book. Give suggestions about how to read effectively. You may refer to the suggestions given in this unit, but contribute your own ideas, too. Do not plagiarize *The Real Thing*!

5. Imagine that a friend of yours who has never been to the United States has applied for admission and been accepted at an American college. Your friend has asked you for advice. Write your friend a letter explaining what will be expected.

Unit 3

Overcoming Communication Anxiety
a Speech-Communication Lecture
by
Ray Collins

I. Listening Strategies

Most successful college students follow the familiar motto, "Be prepared." How can you be prepared for Ray Collins' lecture? First, study its title. Check the dictionary for any words in it that you do not know.

It is human nature to listen harder to something that interests us. If you are not already curious about a subject, try answering these questions to increase your motivation to learn it:

a. What questions do you have about the subject? As the lecture develops, listen for answers to your questions. List at least two questions that you hope Ray Collins will answer:

1. _____

2. _____

b. How can you benefit from the information – personally, academically, or both? List at least two ways you could benefit from knowing how to overcome communication anxiety:

1. _____

2. _____

c. Do you already know something about this subject? If so, you may find the information easier to understand, because you have some familiarity with the subject. List at least two things you know about overcoming communication anxiety:

1. _____

2. _____

II. Comprehend the Lecture

Listen attentively to the lecture, and answer the following questions.

Whenever you need more time, stop the tape. Rewind it if you want to hear a section again. Listen to the lecture as many times as you wish.

1. List three elements in the study of speech:

_____

2. What is most speakers' major concern?

_____

3. What is a minor concern?_____

4. The lecturer uses the idiom, "You're old salts." From context, guess

what he means:_____

5. On the psychological scale of anxiety, where does the fear of death

rank? _____

6. Where does Professor Collins say the fear of speaking in front of a

group of people ranks? _____

7. Name at least four symptoms of this fear: _____

_____

8. When you speak, what is on display? _____

9. From context, guess what the lecturer means when he refers to some speakers being "thin-skinned":

_____

10. What is the key to managing anxiety?_____

11. What is the first suggestion the lecturer makes for getting control?

_____

12. What attitude does he encourage speakers to have?

_____

_____

13. When addressing a group of people, what should you look for?

_____

14. What can a speaker do to eliminate some of the energy created by

anxiety? _____

15. What anxiety does the lecturer describe in addition to speaking?

_____

16. What does Professor Collins call people's behavior when they alternately listen and then do not?_____

17. What is the name for listening to yourself?

_____

18. What is the name for listening to a speaker?

_____

19. What kind of remark might a speaker make that could cause a listener to stop paying attention?_____

20. What else might cause the listener to stop paying attention?

_____

21. What is the key to both speaking and listening?

_____

III. Build Vocabulary

You will find these common prefixes useful in determining the meaning of many new words:

1. *intra-*: within. For example, *intracommunication* means talking to (or "within") yourself. Give an example of another word beginning with "intra":

_____

2. *inter-*: between. For example, *intercommunication* occurs

between people. Give an example of another word beginning with "inter":

_____

3. *pre-*: before. For example, "prejudging" means evaluating people before they have a chance to prove themselves. Give an example of a word beginning with "pre":

_____

IV. Summarize

Write a summary of this lecture. It should be about ten to twelve sentences long. Use your own words, paraphrasing what the lecturer has said.

V. Discuss

A. Give an Oral Summary

What qualities should a good oral summary have? Make a list on the board, remembering to consider issues of content as well as delivery.

If you have already written a summary of Ray Collins' lecture, put it aside. Make a list of his key points. Don't write complete sentences.

The lecture lasts about fifteen minutes. Referring to your list, give a tthree-minute summary of the lecture, either to a partner in class, or at home using a tape recorder. Your instructor will decide how many students will present their summaries to the class.

Referring to the criteria that the class generated for evaluating an oral summary, listeners will write comments about the summaries, noting two strengths and one weakness of each one. The teacher will review the listeners' comments, and then share them with the speakers.

B. Give a Speech

Using Ray Collins' suggestions for controlling your speaking anxiety, give one of these three types of speeches. To prepare, practice your speech as much as you can. Tape it and listen back; talk into a mirror; give the speech to your friends, family or pet; mentally rehearse your speech as you take a walk, jog or drive.

Unless your instructor tells you otherwise, make your speech last from 3 - 5 minutes.

1. Speak to inform

Choose a subject you know well, and educate your listeners about it. You may want to narrow a topic from these general suggestions:

a. Explain how to do something, like choose a major, change a tire, overcome a fear, play soccer, find a bargain or register for college.

b. Describe a special place you've visited, such as a national or local park, historical site, theme park, museum or art gallery.

c. Explain how something works, such as a computer program, the mind of a toddler, the human circulatory system or the organization at a workplace.

d. Tell about a famous American such as a political leader, an author, scientist, reformer or athlete.

2. Speak to persuade

Choose a subject you know well, and convince your listener that your opinion is valid. You may want to narrow a topic from these general suggestions:

a. Defend one side of a controversy, such as abortion, capital punishment, gun control or population control.

b. Pretend you are a salesperson, and your audience is your potential buyer. Convince your listeners to buy what you have to offer. Keep in mind that they don't like to waste their money.

3. *Tell a story*

Choose a story you know well, and tell it to your listeners. Do not memorize the story word for word from a book; tell it your own way. Be sure the story is not already familiar to your audience, or make up your own. Here are some suggestions:

a. A fairy tale, fable, legend or myth

b. A short story you have read (or made up yourself)

c. A favorite children's night-time story

C. Listen to the Speeches

Remember Ray Collins' tips about overcoming listening anxiety. Take notes during each speech to help you remember what has been said. At the end of the speech, review your notes. The instructor will select a few students after each speech to give a one-minute summary of it. Or, students may be asked to write a short summary of it.

D. Conduct an Interview

1. Your instructor may assign each student a particular individual to interview on campus or in the community. Find out as much as you can about the person so that you will be knowledgeable when you plan your questions for the interview.

If you select the person to interview, you might choose someone according to one of these criteria:

a. someone who is important

b. someone who is especially interesting

c. someone whom you admire

       d. someone who has information you and your classmates

          would like to learn

2. Determine what you want to find out during the interview. For example, are you interested in the person's knowledge of a career, skills, or travel experience? Be clear about your interview's purpose.

3. Make an appointment for the interview, and check to be sure you can bring a tape recorder with you. Prepare a list of questions that will elicit the information you want.

4. With a partner in class, practice asking your questions. Revise them if appropriate.

5. During the interview, remember that your job is to listen and to ask questions.

6. After the interview, listen to your recorded version. Summarize the most interesting and pertinent information from the tape, and report it to the class. Be prepared to answer questions of your classmates.

VI. Write

Any of the speech topics in *IV. Discuss*, or the interview, can be developed in writing.

Unit 4

Supply and Demand
an Economics Lecture
by
Dan McUsic

I. Know What to Note

When class begins, have your notebook and pen ready. First, write the date. If the professor says there will be a quiz "on the material covered last week," you need to know which material that was.

Listen actively, deciding what's important and worth writing down. Don't trust your memory! Be sure to write something down if:

- the instructor writes it on the board.
- it gets repeated.
- it's a definition.
- it's a statistic.
- the instructor says it's "important," "fundamental," "major," "key" or "significant."

To speed your note-taking, abbreviate whenever possible. Here are some common symbols, but you will create your own, too:

*	key idea, main point	↑ (↓)	increases (decreases)
=	equals, is	*c/w*	compared with
≈	about equal to	*w/*	with
≠	not equal to	*w/o*	without
<	smaller than	→	causes, becomes
>	greater than	*ex.*	for example
∴	therefore	*etc.*	plus more examples
?	a reminder to find out what a word or idea means		

Underline sentences or words that seem especially important so you can spot them easily when you review.

Indent examples or explanations of main ideas, almost like an outline. That way, you're organizing the material as you note it.

Another time-saver is to omit unimportant words. Do not write whole sentences if a phrase is clear.

II. Sample Lecture Notes

Here is an example of notes based on Dan McUsic's economics class. Read them as you listen to the lecture. After the lecture, answer the questions about the notes. Listen to the lecture as many times as you wish.

Supply and Demand
Wednesday, September 25

✱ *Laws of Supply and Demand key to economics*

Supply = various amts. of part. good or service that <u>producer</u> (business, corp., those making products or providing services) is willing to make avail. to marketplace at a part. $ and time.

Demand = various amts. of part. good or service that <u>consumer</u> (one who buys) is willing to purchase at a part. $ and time.

(true for <u>both goods + services</u>)

<u>now U.S. = a service-oriented econ.</u>
   manuf. jobs lost due to new tech + countries with cheaper labor
   now : service econ., for ex., major income sources = tourism in Haw., Cal and Fl
   before: in Detroit, a h.s. diploma → good paying job on assembly line building cars, more $ than h.s. teacher!
   Now ≠ the case, because auto factories → Mex., Korea, Taiwan, or closed,
   ? or <u>robotics</u> do the work

Law of Supply = as price increases, quantity brought to marketplace also increases

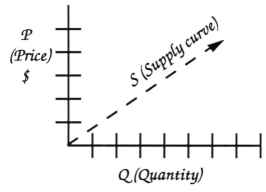

profit motive = self-interest (it's 'common sense') = make the product that's bringing the most money!

Law of demand = as price goes down, quantity goes up.
ex. If something I normally buy is on sale, I purchase more than usual to take advantage of cheap price.

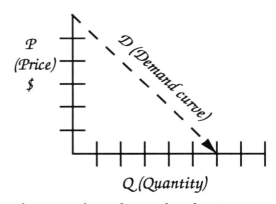

next time = how do these 2 laws work in the marketplace?
compromise between objectives of suppliers and consumers =
? _equilibrium point_

III. Recognize Notetaking Strategy

1. Why has the student written the date?

2. List three abbreviations, and what they stand for, that the notetaker uses in the definition of "supply":

_____

_____

_____

3. Why do you suppose the words "producer" and "consumer" are underlined?

_____

4. Explain why the notes say "both goods & services" even though the definitions already written include those words:

_____

5. Why do you suppose that the student has indented ideas listed under the heading "Now U.S. = a service-oriented econ."?

_____

6. Why do you suppose the student has question marks by "robotics"

and   "equilibrium"?   _____

_____

7. To be well prepared for the next lecture, the student should review these notes enough times to be able to define terms even when looking away from the note page. If the student has any questions about the material, what do you recommend?

_____

IV. Summarize

Write a summary of this lecture. It should be about ten to twelve sentences long. Use your own words, paraphrasing what the lecturer has said.

V. Discuss

1. By reviewing these notes, the student can see the main points of the lecture. What the lecturer emphasizes is likely to be the focus of a quiz. Practice predicting what might be asked on a quiz.

    a. In small groups, list at least four terms or ideas that a student might be asked to define on a quiz. Referring to your notes, have a group recorder write out the definitions.

    b. Do you think students might be asked to reproduce the graph? Why or why not? Be prepared to explain the reasons for your answer.

    c. The lecturer gives several examples illustrating his assertion that the U.S. is now a service-oriented economy. In a quiz, students might be asked to list examples of services. In your groups, list as many examples as you can. You might set a timer and see which group can come up with the most examples in the time allotted.

2. What are the main goods and services produced in the area where you are now living? If most students are new to the area, your instructor may ask you to conduct research about the local economy. Report back to the class. For example, the instructor might ask some students to research the main employers in the area, or the newest businesses, or the history of selected ones. Sources of information might be your school and public libraries, the Chamber of Commerce, and the businesses themselves. If you interview a business person, keep in mind the interviewing and speaking tips listed in Unit 3.

3. Have small groups each select a good or service to study. Then,

research a change in supply and demand for the good or service. Report what you have learned to the class as a whole. Include:

- the name of the product or service
- a description of the change, including dates
- the cause of the change
- the effect of the change
- today's situation
- your group's prediction for the future

4.   Professor McCusic says that next time he will talk about the "equilibrium point." Because the notes have a question mark by "equilibrium," the student plans to check the word in the dictionary; it means "a balance."

The professor will probably begin the next class by defining the term again. He might ask if any students can explain what it means, using a specific example to illustrate the idea.

On the board, list criteria for evaluating answers. Then, have each student write a brief explanation of equilibrium point and an example on a slip of paper. Do not write your names. It's okay to use the lecture notes to help you. Have volunteers read the explanations aloud, either in small groups or to the whole class, depending on its size.

Discuss the various explanations, evaluating them according to the criteria developed.

VI. Write

1. Topics 2 through 4 in *V. Discuss* can be developed in writing.

2. Describe an example in your own life in which the laws of supply and demand have affected your decision making.

Unit 5

Marketing
a Business Lecture
by
Madelaine Wolfe

I. Take Notes During the Lecture

Watch the lecture, taking notes as conscientiously as you can. To keep up with the lecturer, be selective in what you write down. Do not try to write everything that she says. Abbreviate, use symbols and omit unimportant words. To organize the information, indent and underline as you note. If you need more time to write, stop the tape. Listen to the lecture as many times as you wish.

Answer the following questions by referring to your notes. If necessary, watch the lecture again and add to your notes.

1. What manufactured product does the lecturer use for her example?

_____

2. What is the purpose of the day's discussion?_____

_____

3. What is the lecturer's guess about the students and their parents?

_____

4. For Americans working overseas, what is the only area of

employment larger than sales?_____

5. What group constitutes the largest growing segment of American

salespeople?   _____

6. What quality about the packaging of a product does the lecturer

emphasize?   _____

7. By what means might a product such as a computer be shipped?

_____

8. How are many liquid products transported?_____

9. If a computer is not immediately sold, what happens to it?

_____

10. What marketing term is often used for "shipping"?_____

_____

11. In what academic discipline related to marketing would you study

supply and demand?   _____

12. What happens if inventory levels aren't controlled, and supply goes

above demand?_____

13. Who buys from retailers?_____

14. What is the main difference between a wholesaler and a retailer?

_____

15. Who does the wholesaler usually sell to?_____

16. In what academic discipline related to marketing would you study

techniques that sell products effectively?_____

17. What final definition of marketing does the lecturer give?

_____

_____

18. By what process does Apple get the parts needed to manufacture its

computer?   _____

19. What occupation does Professor Wolfe use as an example to show
the role of marketing where we would not normally think of it?

_____

II. Recognize Key Points

Review your notes after each lecture. Underline or highlight new
terms. If the lecturer does not define a word that is new to you, ask her
to explain it.

Although the dictionary may give a general definition for a word, a
college course may use that word in only one specific sense. For
example, Madelaine Wolfe gives an extended definition of marketing;
the dictionary might simply define marketing as "selling," and that
definition would not suffice in this college course.

Check your notes for marketing terms identified in the lecture. The
professor has written them on the board, emphasizing that they are
important and you should include them in your study.

To review for a quiz, create and study your own flash cards: put the
term on one side, and the definition on the other. Try doing this
matching exercise, using your notes or flash cards to help you.

Directions: In the blank provided, write the letter of the definition
on the right that best matches each term listed on the left.

_____ 1. warehouse   A. store that sells to individuals

_____ 2. wholesaler   B. boxes, plastic covers

_____ 3. retailer   C. a business that sells large quantities

_____ 4. packaging   D. shipping

_____ 5. advertising   E. activities to increase demand

_____ 6. distribution   F. what buyers want

_____ 7. end user   G. means of transporting some liquids

_____ 8. pipeline   H. consumer

_____ 9. demand   I. place for storing goods

_____10. economics   J. study of supply & demand

III. Summarize

Write a summary of this lecture. It should be about ten to twelve sentences long. Use your own words, paraphrasing what the lecturer has said.

IV. A Sample Quiz

The instructor gives this quiz after her lecture on marketing:

List at least three examples of buyers, and three examples of sellers.

To prepare for a quiz, it is important to study your notes. However, to perform well during the quiz, you must do more than recall your notes. Consider carefully what the quiz asks you to do. <u>You must</u>

<u>answer the question asked</u>. This sounds simple, but some students receive low quiz scores because they fail to read the question carefully or understand what it demands. The low scores do not accurately reflect how well they know the material. When you take a quiz, begin by studying the directions. Underline key words. For example:

<u>*List*</u> *at least* <u>*three examples*</u> *of buyers,* <u>*and*</u> *three examples of sellers.*

Carefully consider what you are being asked to do:

- *List* means to write words or phrases, not complete sentences or paragraphs.
- *Three examples* means three specific cases, not general ideas.
- *And* tells you to give examples of both buyers and sellers.

Another quiz might not ask for a list. Each of these common direction words requires a different response:

- *analyze* (take it apart, divide it into pieces)
- *compare* (show similarities)
- *contrast* (show differences)
- *define* (explain what something means)
- *describe* (make a picture in words)
- *evaluate* (identify the good and the bad)
- *justify* (defend)

V. Discuss

1. In small groups, select at least two of the direction words from the list under *IV. A Sample Quiz.* On a piece of paper, compose quiz questions based on this lecture using the two direction words. Have groups exchange questions, and then prepare appropriate answers to them, either aloud or in writing. You may use your notes.

2. Look around the room. Have each student write on a slip of paper the name of something that is in the room as a result of marketing. Put your names on the back of the slips, and place them in a basket or hat. Have volunteers read the slips aloud (without names) and explain

how that object fits in the marketing channel. If they can't, the writers must do so.

3.   Role play the experience of a farmer in the marketing channel. Students can create and act the parts of marketing people whom the farmer might interact with, such as people who sell fertilizer, various kinds of farm equipment, fencing, etc. Use your imagination. Perhaps you might even have competing sellers try to get the farmer's business.

4. In small groups, have each person describe an example of marketing that s/he's seen. For instance, if your family owns a store, or someone you know is a salesperson, or you have worked in a warehouse, explain how that example fits into the marketing channel. Select one person from each group to summarize for the class what the group members described.

VI. Write

1. All of the topics under *V. Discuss* can be adapted and developed in writing.

2.   Design an advertising campaign for a product or service that you identify. Write up a proposal for your campaign to be submitted to the marketing department of the company.

3. Write a letter to a friend or family member explaining to the person how his/her job fits into the marketing channel.

4. Write a paper in which you explain the marketing process. Use an American service as your main example.

5.   Look around your study area and select an object that you consider important. Explain the role of marketing in causing that object to be where it is now.

Unit 6

The Essay
an English Lecture
by
Reginald Lockett

I. Comprehend the lecture

Watch the lecture, taking notes as conscientiously as you can. If you need more time to write, stop the tape. Listen to the lecture as many times as you wish.

Answer the following questions by referring to your notes. If necessary, watch the lecture again and add to your notes.

1. What is the purpose of an essay? _____

_____

2. What does the American *linear* method mean?_____

_____

3. A paragraph usually has a topic _____, three

specific supports and a _____ topic sentence.

4. If a paragraph is compared to a toddler, what might an essay be

compared to? _____

5. Define *thesis*:_____

6. What does the blueprint do?_____

_____

7. What does the motivator do?_____

_____

8. What is the function of a topic sentence in each central paragraph of

an essay?   _____

_____

9. What type of support can be used in a central paragraph?

_____

10. What should be in the conclusion? _____

_____

11. Should any of these rules for essay writing in an English class be

changed for essays in other subjects?_____

_____

12. When should you compose the title? _____

_____

II. Respond to the Lecture

A. Draw Analogies

An analogy demonstrates a similarity in a relationship. It is often
written like this:

A topic sentence : a paragraph = a thesis : an essay

This analogy says that the relationship between a topic sentence and a paragraph is the same as the relationship between a thesis and an essay. It should be read like this: "A topic sentence is to a paragraph as a thesis is to an essay." In other words, the opinion asserted in the topic sentence is supported in the paragraph, just as the opinion asserted in the thesis is supported in the essay.

Because analogies help us to understand concepts, writers and speakers often use them. To improve your ability to see similarities between relationships, complete these analogies by filling in each blank with the most appropriate word:

1. paragraph : essay = _____: adolescent

2. reworded topic sentence : paragraph = _____:

   essay

3. carrot : donkey = motivator: _____

4. summer : winter = spring:_____

5. parent : child = teacher: _____

6. instrument : musician = _____: driver

7. blouse : woman = _____: man

8. artist : painting = _____: essay

9. bear : woods = _____: water

10. horse : _____ = typewriter : computer

B. Opinion vs. Fact

A thesis asserts an arguable opinion. It is subjective, expressing a belief. In contrast, objective ideas are not arguable; they are true or false, open to verification. The essay writer supports or defends the thesis by means of facts, examples or comments by experts.

Here are some examples of facts and opinions:

fact: At 3:00 p.m. it was sunny, 75° and the wind was calm.
opinion: It was a beautiful afternoon.

fact: Jaime Romero is a college freshman.
opinion: Jaime Romero is destined for a great future.

Directions: Label each sentence below as *fact* or *opinion*. You may want to discuss this exercise with a partner or in small groups.

_____1. Chocolate ice cream is more satisfying than vanilla.

_____2. Wynton Marsalis is the greatest trumpet player that ever lived.

_____3. Wynton Marsalis plays both jazz and classical music.

_____4. The San Francisco '49ers are a football team.

_____5. The '49ers don't stand a chance against the Miami Dolphins.

_____6. Writing a good essay is easy if you're smart.

_____7. John F. Kennedy was a wonderful U.S. President.

_____8. Gambling is legal in the state of Nevada.

_____9. Gambling is illegal in the state of Nebraska.

_____10. Gambling is fun.

III. Summarize

Write a summary of this lecture. It should be about ten to twelve sentences long. Use your own words, paraphrasing what the lecturer has said.

IV. Discuss

1. Have each student create an analogy. On a slip of paper, write three of its four parts. Draw a blank line where the fourth belongs. Have each student put his/her analogy in a basket. Other students each draw a slip from the basket; on the board, write the complete analogy. Be sure you can explain how the analogy you created makes sense.

2. Get into small groups. Have each group compose an opinion about the classroom you are in, and list at least five facts that could be used to support the opinion. Then, have a spokesperson from each group read the group's opinion and supporting facts aloud to the rest of the class. Have any groups used the same facts to support different opinions?

3. Choose a major event in the news, and have each student bring to class a newspaper account of it. Compare the versions, and determine what information is factual, and what is opinion. (You could also do this with historical accounts of a past event, or reviews of a movie, or explanations of a traffic accident.)

4. The introductory paragraph of an essay should contain a motivator to make the reader interested in the topic of the essay. The motivator might be an anecdote, humorous story or striking statement that has something to do with the topic.

Your instructor will give you a general topic area, such as an issue of current interest, a controversy, something about the college or your academic program, something about your class or community, etc. In small groups, compose a one-sentence thesis about that topic. Then compose a motivator that would interest a reader in your essay. Have a spokesperson for your group read the motivator and thesis to the rest of the class.

5. Select a thesis sentence composed for question 4, and have students in small groups write topic sentences for at least three central paragraphs of an essay that could be used to support the thesis. (You can make up information if necessary.) Have a recorder from each group write the topic sentences on the board.

V. Write

1. Topics 2 through 5 in *IV. Discuss* can be adapted and developed as essays.

2. List the steps involved in writing an essay. Then, write an essay in which you explain how to write an essay.

3. Assert a thesis about your major, or your career choice, or your college. In an essay, defend your thesis.

4. Imagine that you are filling out a college application with these directions: "What one adjective best describes you? In an essay, explain why."

5. What do you hope to get out of your college education? Write an essay that explains your answer.

6. Try writing two different descriptions of an event (such as a car accident, something in the news, an interaction with a family member or friend, etc.). In one, report objectively, focusing on the facts; do not divulge your opinion. In the other, be subjective, making value judgments and emphasizing your opinion.

Unit 7

Immigration
a History Lecture
by
Dale Debold

I. Comprehend the lecture

Watch the lecture, taking notes as conscientiously as you can. If you need more time to write, stop the tape. Listen to the lecture as many times as you wish.

Answer the following questions by referring to your notes. If necessary, watch the lecture again, and add to your notes.

1. American society is mixed; it is *heterogeneous*. In contrast, what adjective describes a society composed of people who are all the same?

_____

2. Before the American Revolution in 1776, what percent of the people

in the British colonies were not English? _____

3. What is the main benefit to the United States resulting from immigration?

_____

4. In Dale Debold's opinion, what happens to homogeneous countries?

_____

5. What factor regarding immigrants does Professor Debold say has the unusual feature of not needing to be qualified (or limited)?

_____

6. What is the name for the basic reason why people might leave their

country of birth? _____

7. List four conditions that might motivate people to leave their native

country:_____

_____

_____

_____

8. What is the name for immigrants' belief that in a different land they will have an opportunity for a better life?

_____

9. In the 18th Century, the United States was the first society ever to

have no official _____.

10. In what way do immigrants differ from their compatriots who do

not leave their country of birth? _____

_____

11. Between what years was the "Century of Immigration"?

_____

12. What events in Europe and the United States mark the beginning

of that century? _____

_____

13. What legislation in the United States ended that century?

_____

14. How many Europeans settled in the United States during that

century?_____

15. What is the first big contribution that immigrants have made to

American society? _____

16. What country preceded America's industrialization by fifty years?

_____

17. By the beginning of World War I, what percent of the world's

industrial production was in the United States?_____

18. What is the second big contribution that immigrants have made to

American society?_____

19. What key value have immigrants given to native-born Americans?

_____

20. Every generation, American society changes; in other words, it is

constantly_____.

21. Name and define the friction sometimes caused by immigration:

_____

22. Give an example of a mild form of nativism:_____

_____

23. During what decade was the the Ku Klux Klan (KKK) guilty of

violence against immigrants?_____

24. What happens to nativism over time? _____

_____

25. How do immigrants prove themselves to native-born Americans?

_____

_____

II. Respond to the Lecture

A. Study Your Notes

In order to learn, you have to do more than write good notes. You also have to study them. How should you study your lecture notes? Here is a list of possibilities:

1. Recopy your notes, putting hastily written ideas into a well-organized outline.

2. Scan your notes until you come to a key idea. Aloud, explain every key idea, first using your notes to help you, and then without looking at them.

3. List terms and define them, giving at least one example of each.

4. Write a paragraph summarizing an important section of the lecture.

5. Imagine that a friend absent from class has asked you what s/he missed. Tell your friend what the lecture covered.

B. Predict Essay Questions

Dale Debold uses the word "key" to emphasize the most important themes in his lecture. Check your notes. The first key he identifies is that "Immigration is the key to American society." This assertion is an opinion which could be the thesis of an essay. A likely quiz or exam topic would be based on a key theme. Here is a typical topic:

In an essay, show how immigration is the key to American society.

Fill in the blanks in this outline for the essay. Each Roman numeral represents a paragraph in the essay.

I. *Introduction, with thesis:* Immigration is the _____ to American society.

II. *Topic sentence:* Immigrants have contributed_____ that has developed the U.S. economy.

III. *Topic sentence:* Immigrants have contributed_____ that has affirmed positive aspects of American society that pulled immigrants here.

IV. *Topic sentence:* Most importantly, immigrants have provided new

_____ to native-born Americans that have prompted this country constantly to remake itself.

V. *Conclusion, with reworded thesis:* Immigration

_____ the United States by making it a dynamic, self-renewing society.

To prepare for an essay test, look for opinions that the lecture material would allow you to support or discuss. For example, Professor

Debold emphasizes his opinion that America is strengthened by immigrants' new perspectives. Consider the opposing opinion: nativists oppose immigration, fearful that newcomers will weaken America. A likely essay topic might require that you present both views. For example,

In an essay, contrast the attitude of nativism with the notion that immigration strengthens American society.

Predict test questions, making a list of possibilities. Then, compose a thesis for each one. Determine what support you could use to defend each thesis, first by reviewing your notes, and then without looking at them.

III. Summarize

Write a summary of this lecture. It should be about ten to twelve sentences long. Use your own words, paraphrasing what the lecturer has said.

IV. Discuss

1. The United States was the first society not to have an official religion. Consider the advantages and disadvantages of this un-precedented freedom. You might present a panel discussion, a debate, or simply discuss the issue.

2. Interview immigrants. In preparation, the class will make a list of questions about issues such as the push/pull factor and the immigrants' attitudes toward risk-taking. If you are not able to interview immigrants to the United States, interview people who have recently come to your city, your neighborhood, your school or workplace. Present oral summaries of your interviews to the class.
   If you are an immigrant, you may describe your own experience.

3. A good way to remember new ideas is to relate them to yourself and what you already know. The lecturer mentions that immigrants are risk-takers. Most Americans have ancestors who left their countries of birth in order to take a chance on a new and better life in the United States.

Are you a risk-taker? Get a partner, and ask each other these questions. Write the number of the answer below that most closely matches your partner's response to each question.

yes, sure	*5*
probably	*4*
maybe	*3*
slight chance	*2*
never!	*1*

Would you ...

_____1. try skydiving?

_____2. invite a classmate of the same sex to go with you to a movie?

_____3. travel to a country whose language you don't speak?

_____4. try a new food offered by a friend (you don't know what's in it)?

_____5. teach this class a song you know, just for fun?

_____6. have a pet snake?

_____7. drive a friend's new car?

_____8. ride in a space shuttle?

_____9. write a poem?

_____10. read your poem to this class?

Add up your numbers. If you totaled more than 40 points, you enjoy risk!

4. What does *risk* mean to you? On a slip of paper, have each person anonymously write a one-sentence definition of *risk*. Mix up the definitions, and then have volunteers read them aloud. Can a definition that is generally valid be inferred?

5. To become more familiar with the perspectives of nativists and immigrants, plan a debate between the two viewpoints. You may do some research in the library. In small groups, list the arguments each side would be likely to present. Taking turns, proceed with the debate.

V. Write

1. Write an essay on either topic in *IIB. Predict Essay Questions.* Base your essay on your lecture notes, adding your own opinion if you wish.

2. All but topic 3 under *IV. Discuss* can be developed as essays.

3. Has your definition of "risk" changed over time? If so, what did you used to consider a "risk"? What is risky for you now, but you expect will not be so in the future?

4. In an essay assess the push/pull factor in an aspect of your life. For example, you might discuss what has pushed you from your former life and pulled you to college.

5. Have any of your ancestors been immigrants? If so, research the life of your ancestor, or the era in which s/he immigrated.

6. Some people claim that a country that changes with each new generation is stronger than a country that remains essentially the same generation after generation. In an essay, explain your view.

7. Would you prefer living in a heterogeneous society (one with people having different languages and cultural backgrounds living together) or in a homogeneous one? In an essay, explain your answer.

Unit 8

Culture
a Sociology Lecture
by
Phil Crawford

I. Comprehend the Lecture

Watch the lecture, taking notes as conscientiously as you can. If you need more time to write, stop the tape. Listen to the lecture as many times as you wish.

Answer the following questions by referring to your notes. If necessary, watch the lecture again and add to your notes.

1. Define *culture*:_____

_____

2. Define *society*:_____

_____

3. Define *cultural universal*:_____

_____

4. Give three examples of cultural universals:_____

_____

5. What do we call society's formal and most severely enforced rules of

behavior? _____

6. When informal folkways are not followed, what is the result?

_____

7. Besides punishment, what else can *sanctions* be? _____

_____

8. In general, a society_____

compliance, and _____ noncompliance.

9. A society's _____ are what people hold

to be important and good, or not important and bad.

10. Define *subculture*: _____

_____

11. Give two examples of subcultures in the United States:

_____

_____

12. Define *culture shock*: _____

_____

13. Summarize two examples of culture shock that are described by

Professor Crawford: _____

_____

_____

_____

14. Define *ethnocentrism*: _____

_____

15. Define *cultural relativism*: _____

_____

16. Briefly describe the example the lecturer gives about kissing as a

culturally relative behavior: _____

_____

17. Briefly describe the Los Angeles judge's decision, and his reason for

it: _____

_____

_____

_____

18. What groups criticized the Judge's decision? _____

19. Why did they criticize it? _____

_____

20. Define *bilingual education*: _____

_____

21. What is the attitude of some opponents of bilingual education?

_____

_____

22. What is the antithesis of bilingual education?

_____

23. Will students be expected to read Chapter 4 for next time, or not until after the lecturer has talked about English immersion?

_____

II. Respond to the lecture

A. The Lecturer's Expectations

1. Phil Crawford begins his lecture by asking if any student can define _culture_. When no one responds, he says, "I can see that we all read the material very carefully in preparation for the day's assignment." Although he is smiling, he is sarcastic, saying the opposite of what he means. Because no one answers his question, he assumes the students have not done the assigned reading.

What might he do to prompt students to be better prepared? He could give a quiz, and unprepared students will receive low grades. The quiz itself could be a demonstration of a sociological principle he explains: noncompliance with a rule (in this case, to be prepared for class) results in a punishment (a low quiz grade).

To avoid negative sanction, comply with a teacher's expectation. Read an assigned chapter carefully, and be ready to provide definitions from it. (If the lecturer does not give a quiz, you can show him or her that you are prepared by answering questions. If you do not volunteer a response, the lecturer may assume that you have not done the assignment.) You may want to review Unit 2's suggestions on how to read a text.

B. Vocabulary Development through Word Parts

1. *subculture*: "Sub-" is a prefix meaning "below." In this sociology class, "subculture" means "a small part of a dominant society." Write at least two other words in which "sub" means "below":

1. _____

2. _____

2. *ethnocentrism*: "Ethno-" refers to a group of people defined by their racial, national or religious characteristics. Some "hyphenated Americans" are identified by their ethnic identity, such as Mexican-American or Japanese-American. "Centrism" means being "focused on the self."

Everyone is a member of some ethnic group. Of what group are you a member?

_____

C. Thesis and Antithesis

Professor Crawford concludes by saying that English immersion is the "antithesis of bilingual education." From context, you can guess that *antithesis* means the *opposite*. Take the word apart: "anti" means "against." "Thesis" means a "statement of an idea or opinion."

A controversy can often be described in terms of a thesis and its antithesis. For example,

Thesis: Beating one's wife for infidelity is appropriate.
Antithesis: Beating one's wife for infidelity is not acceptable.

Directions: Compose an antithesis for each thesis given below:

1. Thesis: Eating dog meat is disgusting.

Antithesis: _____

2. Thesis: Kissing is a pleasurable, positive behavior.

   Antithesis: _____

3. Thesis: In American schools, children should learn in their native languages.

   Antithesis: _____

   _____

4. Thesis: Abortion should be against the law.

   Antithesis: _____

5. Thesis: High school attendance should be optional.

   Antithesis: _____

   _____

III. Apply Concepts

A. On a Quiz

To do well in college, you need to do more than memorize objective information; you must also recognize and apply concepts. For example, in this sociology course you might be asked to identify cultural concepts illustrated by people's behavior. Or you might be asked to give your own examples of the concepts Professor Crawford explained.

Refer to your notes as you complete this quiz which requires that you apply some of the concepts covered in the lecture.

Directions: Fill in each blank using the term below that best describes the behavior.

cultural universal   *ethnocentrism*

negative sanction   *culture shock*

cultural relativism   *subculture*

1. A woman refuses to cross the street because the sign shows a man walking.

_____

2. Books comparing various cultures nearly always have a chapter on body adornment.

_____

3. "People from my part of the country speak with the correct accent!"

_____

4. In contrast with the larger society, hippies of the 1960s advocated peace and love, not competition and acquisition of material wealth.

_____

5. Kids on the playground laugh at the only child who does not want to join in the baseball game.

_____

B. On an Essay Test

   To prepare for an essay test on the material in this lecture, review your notes for key concepts. Predict how each concept might be the focus of an essay. To prepare for the exam, plan an essay based on the concept.

   For example, Phil Crawford points out that every society has rules governing behavior on a continuum. An essay question might demand that you show your understanding of this concept and can apply it. The question might be:

Use specific examples to show the range of rules and sanctions governing people's behavior within their culture.

Fill in the blanks in this outline for the essay. Each Roman numeral represents a paragraph.

I. *Introduction, with thesis:* Within a culture, a wide range of rules

and sanctions governs people's _____.

II. *Topic Sentence:* The strongest rules are _____ enforced by punishment including imprisonment and fines.

III. *Topic Sentence:* A person's_____ with social rules not considered very important might result in laughter, ridicule or ostracism.

IV. *Topic Sentence:* Compliance with social rules may result in

_____sanctions, such as money, friendship, love and prestige.

V. *Conclusion, with reworded thesis:* There are many ways society prompts its members to comply with its rules, ranging from

strong _____ sanctions against unwanted behavior to strong rewards for behavior deemed good.

IV. Summarize

Write a summary of this lecture. It should be about ten to twelve sentences long. Use your own words, paraphrasing what the lecturer has said.

V. Discuss

1. Have each student review his/her lecture notes and select a key concept, one that might be the focus of an essay question on a test. Using that concept, on a slip of paper compose a thesis. Because a thesis is an opinion, it will be a subjective assertion that an essay could argue.

Put the papers in a basket and have other students draw them. Each student must then explain, in writing or aloud, what the key concept s/he drew from the basket means, and how an essay supporting it might be organized. Use your notes.

2. Professor Crawford describes culture shock, something which most travelers and immigrants have experienced. In small groups, have each person describe any incident of social miscommunication or misunderstanding that s/he has experienced or observed, whether recently or long ago. The instructor will survey the groups and select one or two anecdotes from each to be presented to the class as a whole.

3. If you are enrolled at an American college, undoubtedly many students in your class have had some problem dealing with room-mates, friends or classmates from a different culture. On a slip of paper, have each student write down a problem s/he has experienced due to cultural differences. Do not put any names on the papers. Volunteers will read each one aloud, and the class will suggest ways to solve or reduce the problem described.

If you are not at an American college, describe problems that you think you might encounter in the future, or problems you have had in past interactions with people from another culture.

4. Organize debates. Professor Crawford has raised many controversial issues. Being able to defend an opinion well is essential to success in college, and a debater must consistently support the viewpoint of whichever debate team s/he is on. Listeners will ask questions of the debaters and vote by secret ballot for whichever side has argued the most convincingly.

You may create your own topics, or choose pro/con teams on issues mentioned in the lecture, such as:

- Husbands and wives should have equal power within a marriage.

- People living in one country should all use the same language.

- It is the obligation of immigrants to adopt the cultural values of the dominant society in their new country.

VI. Writing Topics

1. All of the topics in *V. Discuss* can be adapted and developed as essays.

2. If you are a U.S. resident, write an essay describing an aspect of the culture that you particularly like.

   If you are not in the United States, write about a positive aspect of American culture that you have heard or read about.

3. If you have visited or lived in a place with a culture different from your own, write an essay about an aspect of that culture that surprised you. In other words, contrast your expectation with the reality.

   Or, write a letter to someone from a different culture who is about to visit you. In the letter, describe an aspect of your culture that you think might take your visitor by surprise.

4. Complete the essay outlined in *IIIB. On an Essay Test.* Begin the introduction with a motivator that leads to the thesis statement. Provide specific examples to support the topic sentences of each central paragraph.

Unit 9

Interpreting "Borders"
a Humanities Lecture
by
Martha Kendall

I. Read and React to Assignments

The assignment for this lecture is to read "Borders." Read it actively: underline key words, put question marks by words you need to check or ideas you do not understand, and note contrasts or similarities. It is particularly important with poetry to respond both intellectually and emotionally. How does it make you feel? Read the poem several times, aloud as well as silently.

Borders
Pat Mora

My research suggests that men and women may speak different languages that they assume are the same.

Carol Gilligan

> If we're so bright,
> why didn't we notice?
>
> I
>
> The side-by-side translations
> were the easy ones.
> Our tongues tasted *luna*
> chanting, chanting to the words

it touched; our lips circled
moon sighing its longing.
We knew; similar but different.

II

And we knew of grown-up talk,
how even in our own home
like became unlike,
how the child's singsong
          I want, I want
burned our mouth
when we whispered in the dark.

III

But us? You and I
who've talked for years
tossing words back and forth
          success, happiness
back and forth
over coffee, over wine
at parties, in bed
and I was sure you heard,
          u n d e r s t o o d,
though now I think of it
I can remember screaming
to be sure.

So who can hear
the words we speak
you and I, like but unlike,
and translate us to us
side by side?

"Borders" from the book by the same title is reprinted by permission of the Arte Publico Press, University of Houston, Houston, Texas 77204-2090

II. Comprehend the lecture

Watch the lecture, taking notes as conscientiously as you can. If you need more time to write, stop the tape. Listen to the lecture as many times as you wish.

Answer the following questions by referring to your notes. If necessary, watch the lecture again and add to your notes.

1. What does the *Humanities* refer to? _____

_____

2. The Humanities are interdisciplinary. List three academic disciplines

they include: _____

3. Explain what *universal* means with reference to literature:

_____

4. What do poets do with words?_____

_____

5. (yes, no) Does "Borders" have regular rhythm and rhyme?_____

6. Define *epigraph*: _____

7. "Difference" need not imply inferiority or_____.

8. What is the first example of communication problems that Mora's

poem describes?_____

9. Mora is from El Paso, so it is not surprising that she uses the example

of translating between English and_____.

10. Define *connotation*: _____

_____

11. Give three examples of words meaning "fat" that have different

connotations:_____

12. What is the second communication problem that Mora's poem

describes? _____

13. What internal dialog could Mora be referring to?_____

_____

14. What is the third problem the poem describes?_____

_____

15. What happens to words' meanings?_____

16. Give at least three examples of ways speakers can be isolated:

_____

17. Explain "Words are very slippery things."_____

_____

18. What is a positive result of borders? _____

_____

19. Explain "Give me my space."_____

_____

20. "Borders" is based on a metaphor. From context, guess what

metaphor means:_____

III. Respond to the Lecture

A. Connotation

Whereas a scientist strives to use objective language, in the Humanities words may be chosen because of their powerful connotations. Recognizing the attitude conveyed by a particular word can be crucial to understanding the writer's full meaning.

Directions: To practice being sensitive to connotation, arrange the words below in the appropriate categories. For example:

positive	*neutral*	*negative*
a. filled out	overweight	fat
b. slender	thin	scrawny

1. weird, unusual, special

   _____   _____   _____

2. smart, nerd, genius

   _____   _____   _____

3. tanned, lobster-red, sunburned

   _____   _____   _____

4. bland, normal, well-adjusted

   _____   _____   _____

5. eating, pigging out, having a healthy appetite

   _____   _____   _____

6. experienced, old-fashioned, wise

   _____   _____   _____

7. creative, bizarre, original

_____   _____   _____

8. ear-shattering, loud, pleasant

_____   _____   _____

9. challenging, ridiculous, difficult

_____   _____   _____

10. Make up your own three examples:

_____   _____   _____

B. Metaphor

A metaphor compares an abstract idea to something concrete and familiar. Many proverbs are based on metaphor. Consider the following proverbs, determining their literal and figurative meanings.

Example: Grass always looks greener on the other side of the fence.
   Literal meaning: From a distance grass looks more smooth and green than it does close up.
   Figurative meaning: What somebody else has looks better than what I have.

1. The squeaky wheel gets the grease.

   Literal   meaning:_____

_____

   Figurative   meaning: _____

_____

2. Don't judge a book by its cover.

Literal meaning: _____

_____

Figurative meaning: _____

_____

3. All that glitters is not gold.

Literal   meaning:_____

_____

Figurative   meaning: _____

_____

4. Too many cooks spoil the broth.

Literal meaning: _____

_____

Figurative   meaning: _____

_____

5. An ounce of prevention is worth a pound of cure.

Literal meaning: _____

_____

Figurative meaning: _____

_____

6. Don't make a mountain out of a mole hill.

Literal meaning: _____

_____

Figurative meaning: _____

_____

7. A bird in hand is worth two in the bush.

Literal meaning: _____

_____

Figurative meaning: _____

_____

8. While the cat's away, the mice will play.

Literal meaning: _____

_____

Figurative meaning: _____

_____

9. People who live in glass houses shouldn't throw stones.

Literal meaning: _____

_____

Figurative meaning: _____

_____

10. Look before you leap.

Literal   meaning:_____

_____

Figurative   meaning: _____

_____

C. Vocabulary Development through Word Parts

Universal means "true for everyone." *Uni* means "one." *Dialog* means "two speakers exchanging words." *Di* means two.

To learn more number prefixes, fill in the blanks:

prefix	*example*	*your example*
1. uni	universal	_____
2. di (bi)	dialog	_____
3. tri	triple	_____
4. quad	quadrangle	_____
5. penta	pentameter	_____

IV. Summarize

Write a summary of this lecture. It should be about ten to twelve sentences long. Use your own words, paraphrasing what the lecturer has said.

V. Discuss

1. On a slip of paper, have each student write a definition of one of these words: *success, happiness, honor, love, marriage.* Volunteers

will read the definitions aloud. Discuss similarities and differences.

2. If you speak a language in addition to English, translate a proverb common in that language into English. Help your classmates understand its figurative meaning.

3. In some cultures, personal borders may be viewed differently than they are in the United States. If you have had experience in a culture other than American, comment on this idea using specific examples.

4. In small groups, consider this question: "Do you agree that men and women may speak different languages that they assume are the same?" Explain your answer to the class, giving specific examples.

5. Identify at least three examples of words that mean something different when used by speakers who have been separated due to geography, social class, age or education. For example, "young" or "old" may mean different things to a child and a grandparent.

VI. Write

1. Assert a thesis about difficulties you have experienced in translating between two languages. In an essay, explain your point using specific examples.

2. Write an essay about an internal dialog you have had.

3. Write a poem about borders.

4. What is the role of communication in a personal relationship? Assess its significance.

5. Show how the different languages used by women and men reflect and reinforce their roles in society.

6. Write about any of the topics listed under *V. Discuss.*

Unit 10

Central Processing Unit
a Computer Information Systems Lecture
by
Kishan Vujjeni

I. Comprehend the lecture

Watch the lecture, taking notes as conscientiously as you can. If you need more time to write, stop the tape. Listen to the lecture as many times as you wish.

Answer the following questions by referring to your notes. If necessary, watch the lecture again and add to your notes.

1. What does the central processing unit do? _____

_____

2. What human part can the central processing unit be compared to?

_____

3. Write the abbreviation for the central processing unit:_____

4. What are the two main parts of the central processing unit?

_____

_____

5. Name the four functions of the control unit:_____

_____

6. Name the four arithmetic functions of the arithmetic and logic unit:

_____

7. What does the logic unit do? _____

8. What two possible truth values can the logic unit yield?

_____

9. What are the six possible comparisons? (use abbreviations)

_____

10.   What is another name for the main memory?_____

11.   What are the two parts of the memory?_____

_____

12.   What two things are needed to process information?

_____

13. What initials are used to represent *input* and *output*?_____

14. What can the main memory be compared to?_____

15. What does each byte hold? _____

16. How many bytes are in one kilobyte?_____

17. What three ways are programs and data represented in memory?

_____

18. How many bytes are needed to store *JOHN DOE*?_____

19. How many bytes are needed to store *$123.69*? _____

20. How many binary digits does each byte have? _____

21. What does *bit* mean?_____

22. A *bit* is a switch with two values. What are they?_____

23. What is *ASCII code*? _____

_____

II. Respond to the Lecture

A. Human Memory

Kishan Vujjeni gives a great deal of information in his Computer Information Systems class. How do students know what they are expected to learn? First, he calls the CPU the "brain" of the computer, so it is clearly very important. Also, since he has taken the trouble to project the information on the screen, you can assume he wants you to learn it.

When you enroll in a class like this, how can you learn so much information?

Assess your memory, an important part of your central processing unit – your brain. Human memory is often described as having two parts, short-term and long-term. Short-term memory typically lasts for only a few minutes. When our attention is focused on something – a professor, a friend, a map, a song – we remember the information effortlessly. However, experts estimate that in as little as an hour, 90% of the information in our short-term memory is lost.

In order to retain information, you must store it in your long-term memory. To learn more about your long-term memory, see if you can remember this information.

1. What is your address?_____

2. Who was your first schoolteacher?_____

3. What color is your bedroom at home? _____

4. What was your favorite color when you were ten?_____

5. What is your telephone number? _____

6. Who was your high school principal?_____

7. What color clothing did you wear on the first day of last month?

_____

You probably could not answer all the questions. Why do you suppose you have forgotten some of the information? Give two reasons:

_____

_____

How can you retain information in your long-term memory?

1.   Use the information frequently.

Studying once before a test will not put information into your long-term memory. To retain lecture information, repeat it so many times that it becomes as familiar as your address. To repeat it:

a. Make flash cards.

b. Reread your notes.

c. After reading a section of your notes, look away from your notebook. Can you repeat what you have read – mentally, aloud or in writing?   Can you repeat the information fifteen minutes later? An hour later? The next day?

d. Recopy your notes, organizing them into a neat outline.

e. Study with a partner, asking each other questions about the material.

f. Create a mnemonic (pronounced *neMONic*) device, a trick with language that can help you remember. How can you remember a *bit* is a *binary digit*? It's just "a little bit," a short version of the longer <u>bi</u>nary digi<u>t</u>.

g. Create an acronym, a word formed from the initial letters of words in a name or list, such as "HOMES," which contains the first letters of the names of the Great Lakes on the American-Canadian border: <u>H</u>uron, <u>O</u>ntario, <u>M</u>ichigan, <u>E</u>rie and <u>S</u>uperior.

h. <u>Do</u> something with the information. Most people have their own preferred ways of learning. It makes sense to maximize your own style. Ask yourself how you learn, and actively engage in the processes that best suit you.

(1) Some people learn most easily if they visualize. Look at what you want to learn, developing a mental picture of it. You may internalize best by putting information into your brain through your eyes.

(2) Some people learn most easily if they use their hands. Build a three-dimensional model of the information. Compare it to something tangible, that you can touch. Act out the roles of component parts so that you are physically involved with the information. You may learn best from kinesthetic or "hands-on" experience.

(3) Some people learn most easily if they verbalize. Talk to yourself about the information, tape record it or discuss it with a friend. You may learn best by processing information through auditory channels.

2.   *The information is important to you for personal reasons.*

Recognize why lecture information is as important to you as knowing your birthday, for example. If you major in Computer

Information Systems, understanding a CPU is fundamental. Even if you are taking the course only because it is required, learning this information will help you earn a good grade, raise your G.P.A., and possibly qualify for a scholarship!

Perhaps you had misconceptions about how computers operate, or you have felt anxiety about their use. An understanding of computers may make you feel more comfortable with them. Maybe they can help you do your homework, or you can design a computer game to enjoy when you take a study break, or you can maintain a computerized list of your friends' birthdays.

> 3. *The information is necessary for daily life.*

To retain lecture information, recognize that computers are increasingly common, and understanding them is almost as basic as knowing the location of your clothing.

Associate new information with something already familiar. For example, relate new vocabulary to words you already know. Since you know that "bi" means "two," you can remember a *bi*nary digit has *two* values: on and off.

Connect new information with people you know. Most of us recall people better than we recall numbers or facts. The lecturer compares the CPU to the human brain, and the main memory to our mailbox. Develop your own metaphors, comparing a new idea with something or someone you're familiar with.

B. A Short-Answer Quiz

In order to study effectively from your notes, they must be thorough and accurate. Use them to take this quiz, which the lecturer has given his class:

Directions: In the space at the left, write the letter of the best answer.

_____ 1. The Central Processing Unit (CPU) is composed of
two primary units, the arithmetic unit and _____ unit.

    a. memory   b. control   c. operating
    d. files   e. function

_____ 2. In addition to the Central Processing Unit, the processor
unit also contains the computer's _____.

    a. "brain"   b. main memory   c. input devices
    d. output devices   e. disk drives

_____ 3. Sixteen kilobytes (16KB) is approximately how many bytes?

    a. 1.6 million   b. 16 million   c. 166,000
    d. 16,000   e. 1.6 billion

_____ 4. How many bytes are required to represent the following
series of symbols (numbers/special characters)?

            @123.(456)

    a. 6 b. 7 c. 8 d. 9 e. 10

_____ 5. Which is the most widely used character coding system
for microcomputers?

    a. ASCII   b. EBCDIC   c. packed decimal
    d. zoned decimal   e. decimal

_____ 6. Collectively, the steps *fetch instruction, decode instruction,
execute instruction,* and *store results* are called the_____.

    a. execution cycle   b. instruction cycle
    c. machine cycle   d. information cycle
    e. none of the above

Directions: Write short answers to each of these questions:

1. What does the letter "K" stand for when referring to main
memory?

_____

_____

2. Define "bit" and "byte":_____

_____

3. Identify the two components of the central processing unit:

_____

4. List two types of operations performed by the computer:

_____

III. Summarize

Write a summary of this lecture. It should be about ten to twelve sentences long. Use your own words, paraphrasing what the lecturer has said.

IV. Discuss

Review the three learning strategies listed in *IIA. Human Memory* under "*h*. <u>Do</u> something with the information." Then turn your creativity loose. Form small groups of students who think they learn best in similar ways: through visual (seeing), auditory (listening) or kinesthetic (doing) means. The task of each group is to create a way to study any or all of the information in this lecture so that their particular learning style is maximized. Present your study techniques to the whole class.

V. Research

Researchers must be open minded and objective in gathering and summarizing information. For most college papers, students interpret information they've gathered, making clear which are their own original ideas, and which are taken from sources. These steps apply for most college research:

1. *Focus your inquiry.* If you choose your own topic, narrow it so that you can cover it adequately in a paper of the length and scope assigned. Ask one precise question that your research will answer. For example, if the instructor tells you to write a ten-page (typed, double-spaced) research paper on "something related to computers," you might focus on the use of computers in auto manufacturing, the development of home computers, or the invention of a particular computer. Your research questions for these topics might be: "How are computers used in auto manufacturing?" or "How did home computers develop?" or "Who created the first Apple computer, and how did they do it?"

2. *Find information.* Using a computer or card catalog system, seek library sources to answer your research question. Your professor may specify a minimum number of sources. Aim for variety so that you have diverse perspectives and a well-rounded understanding of your topic. You might begin with an encyclopedia for a general overview, and then pursue books, magazines, journals, newspapers, data bases, etc. If appropriate, conduct interviews and watch videotapes or TV documentaries.

3. *Note information about your sources.* In academic research, you must acknowledge the sources of your information. Presenting words or ideas of someone else as if they are your own is plagiarism. Students guilty of plagiarism receive a failing grade for the paper that was plagiarized, and they may also be disqualified from the course.

Most instructors specify the format they want you to use for presenting your information and its sources. With variations depending on whether the source is a complete book, an article within a collection, a magazine article, etc., you will typically need to note for each source: the author, title, city of publication, publisher, date of publication, pages.

4. *Note information about your topic.* How do you know what to write down? Keep in mind the research question you are answering, and stay focused on it.

Usually you will paraphrase, summarizing the information in your own words. If a phrase, sentence or paragraph seems particularly effective or unique, copy it exactly, putting quotation marks around the borrowed words to indicate that they are taken directly from the original. Regardless of whether you paraphrase or quote, be sure to note the page number where you found the information. In your paper, you will credit the source of each piece of borrowed information; to do so, you will need to specify the exact page where you found it.

5. *Organize the information.* Most research papers are long essays in which a thesis is supported by means of information gathered from sources. Prepare an outline that plans the order for your essay. Most research papers conclude with a List of Works Cited, a list of all your information sources, alphabetized by authors' last names.

6. *Write the paper.* Allow time to write several drafts before you type the final version. Follow the format prescribed by your instructor.

VI. Write

1. Research the role of computers in a profession you are considering.

2. Study an aspect of the history of computers. Focus on a stage of their development, or the invention of a particular computer.

3. Research the impact of computers in an industry you choose, such as banking, auto manufacturing, law enforcement or sales.

4. Investigate the controversy about individuals' privacy rights when computerized information is made accessible to marketing firms, credit companies or public agencies.

5. Choose your own topic relating to computers. Formulate a precise research question which your paper will answer.

Unit 11

Statement of Cash Flow
an Accounting Lecture
by
Steven Wong

I. Abbreviate

In order to take effective notes in this information-packed lecture, you must write fast. Using abbreviations will help. You may create your own, but be sure you can recognize them later. For example, many students might abbreviate like this:

financial statements	*$ stmts*
balance sheet	*bal sheet*
accrual numbers	*accrual #s*
operating activities	*oper. act.*
investing activities	*invest. act.*

Create abbreviations for these terms:

tangible equipment _____

financing activities _____

indirect method _____

cash flow _____

accounts payable _____

II. Comprehend the Lecture

Watch the lecture, taking notes as conscientiously as you can. If you need more time to write, stop the tape. Listen to the lecture as many times as you wish.

Answer the following questions by referring to your notes. If necessary, watch the lecture again and add to your notes.

1. What the four main financial statements in the study of accounting?

_____

_____

2. Which statement is prepared first?_____

3. On what period is the income statement prepared?

_____

4. What does the owner's statement of equity do?_____

_____

5. What summarizes the financial position of the company?

_____

6. What does a company's statement of cash flow summarize?

_____

7. Name and define the first major part of the statement of cash flow:

_____

_____

8. Name and define the second major part of the statement of cash

flow:_____

_____

9. Name the three parts of the *tangible* structure of a firm:_____

_____

10. Name the four parts of the *intangible* structure of a firm:_____

_____

11. Name and define the third major part of the statement of cash

flow:_____

_____

12. What are the two methods by which operating activities can be

calculated?_____

13. Which method is preferred by the Financial Accounting Standards

Board, and is taught to students? _____

14. Which method is used by 98% of practicing accountants, and why?

_____

15. Give the formula for cash inflow: _____

_____

16. Name the three elements used to calculate cash outflow:

_____

17. Give the formula for calculating the physical merchandise flow

through   the   business:_____

_____

18. Define *accounts   payable*:_____

_____

19. Give the formula for calculating a company's operating expenses:

_____

_____

_____

20. Give the formula for determining income tax expenses:

_____

_____

III. Respond to the Lecture

A. Budget your Study Time

If a teacher gives this much information in every class, his students will have a huge amount of material to learn. When you enroll in a course like this, review the tips in Unit 10 on how to memorize.

An old saying goes, "Don't put off until tomorrow what you can do today." It is easier to learn a little at a time. Because repetition is the key to most memorization, review and memorize your notes daily. Set a time to study regularly with other students in your class. That way you will be more likely to stick to your review schedule. Also, by discussing the material with other people, you will find the information easier to remember.

B. Anticipate What You Will Be Expected to Know

In describing the process of making a statement of cash flow, Steven Wong has written a great deal on the board; he expects you to learn it. You should be able to describe the process, define terms and give formulas. You are ready for a quiz when you can do all three things without looking at your notes.

In order to teach something, you must understand it well. Could you teach someone how to prepare a statement of cash flow?

III. Summarize

Write a summary of this lecture. It should be about ten to twelve sentences long. Use your own words, paraphrasing what the lecturer has said.

IV. Discuss

Get into small groups. Each group's task is to create a statement of cash flow. Follow these steps:

1. Make up a company name and a product or service that it sells.

2. Make up dollar amounts for each of your company's various operating activities and for income from sales.

3. Make up dollar amounts for each of your company's various investment activities.

4. Make up dollar amounts for each of your company's various financing activities.

5. Apply appropriate formulas and prepare a statement of cash flow.

6. Each group member will write out and sign one part of the statement. Put it on a transparency, and present it on an overhead projector to the class.

V. Write

Imagine that a new Chief Executive Officer at the company where you work has decided to save money by eliminating what s/he perceives to be unnecessary employees. You are an accountant whose job is threatened. In an effort to keep it, write a letter explaining why your job is crucial to the company. Follow this format for a standard business letter.

your number and street
your city, state and zip code

the date

the person you're writing, Chief Executive Officer
the company name
the company's number and street
the company's city, state and zip code

Dear Ms. (or Mr.) _____:

You might begin by saying something like this: "I understand that you are considering eliminating some positions within the company. I am writing to urge you to keep my position as accountant, because my role is crucial to the well being of the company."

In your subsequent paragraph(s), give your reasons. Type the letter and proofread it carefully.

Sincerely,

your name
your position

Unit 12

Logic
a Critical Thinking Lecture
by
Dan Phillips

I. Comprehend the Lecture

Watch the lecture, taking notes as conscientiously as you can. If you need more time to write, stop the tape. Listen to the lecture as many times as you wish.

Answer the following questions by referring to your notes. If necessary, watch the lecture again and add to your notes.

1. What is the most important aspect of logic? _____

2. What famous book says, "In the beginning was the word"?

_____

3. "Logos" is such a powerful concept that if you use it properly, Dan

Phillips says you can create your own _____.

4. What industry often uses illogic?_____

5. Name the process of thought using deductive logic:

_____

6. What symbol from geometry indicates "therefore"? _____

7. Deductive logic is based on reasoning that moves from the general

to the _____.

8. What ancient Greek example of a syllogism does the lecturer give?

_____

_____

_____

9. Who was Socrates? _____

10. Write the "formula" that represents the syllogism:

_____

_____

_____

11. (yes, no) Is its first generalization true? _____

12. (yes, no) Does it draw a valid conclusion?_____

13. In order for a conclusion to be valid, each premise must be

_____

14. Prejudice may start due to a_____ of logic.

15. What kind of logic is the basis of the scientific method?

_____

16. Induction is based in reasoning that moves from the specific to the

_____.

17. What example does a student give of a product advertised using

illogic?_____

18. What hidden assumption does the advertiser hope the consumer

will accept?_____

_____

19. Is the hidden assumption based on a premise that is true or false?

_____

20. Who or what can make you powerful?_____

II. Respond to the Lecture

A. Recognize Hidden Assumptions

Professor Phillips emphasizes that we use logic daily, even though we may do so subconsciously. To raise your awareness of the role of logic in your life, determine the hidden assumption in each of the examples of advertisements given below. The assumptions can be described in this cause/effect pattern: "If p, then q." Indicate whether or not each assumption is valid, and why.
For example:

> *Streamline cigarettes are slim, elegant and classy. Count yourself among the Streamline!*

hidden assumption: <u>If I smoke Streamline cigarettes, then I will be</u>
   <u>slim, elegant and classy.</u>

(yes, no) Is this valid? <u>no</u>

Why? <u>Smoking does not make someone slim, elegant or classy.</u>

1. Strong men need strong styles in their dress shirts. Are you ready for *Stylos*?

hidden assumption: _____

_____

(yes, no) Is this valid? _____

Why? _____

_____

2. People who demand the best, demand "Fresh."

hidden assumption: _____

_____

(yes, no) Is this valid? _____

Why? _____

_____

3. Super Speakers give sophisticated listeners the sounds they have always wanted.

hidden assumption: _____

_____

(yes, no) Is this valid?_____

why? _____

_____

4. With Slim Beauty weight-loss diet, you can finally have the body you always dreamed of.

hidden assumption: _____

_____

(yes, no)   Is this valid? _____

why? _____

_____

5. "Whisper" is the choice perfume for the real woman.

hidden assumption: _____

_____

(yes, no) Is this valid? _____

Why? _____

_____

B. Generalization

Deductive reasoning is based on a premise that states a generalization. Few generalizations are always true. Nearly always they have to be limited, or qualified (like this one). For example, here's a generalization:

Men are taller than women.

This generalization is false, for all men are not taller than all women. Because a qualifier is not used, the assertion is understood to be about all men and all women. It is true that most men are taller than most women, but a logical person must be very careful to base premises and assumptions on generalizations that are always valid. Few assertions are always or never true, or, as the saying goes, "All generalizations are false, including this one."

A stereotype reflects an oversimplified, invalid generalization; prejudice occurs when that generalization is applied to an individual case. For example, lazy thinking might prompt a person to claim, based on one or two negative experiences, that all English teachers are boring. When such a person enrolls in an English class, that person is likely to assume it will be dull, when in fact Professor Jones might be energetic and inspiring. Stereotyping is the misuse of logic, because it builds a syllogism based on a major premise that is not true, as in:

English teachers are boring.
John Jones is an English teacher.
 ∴ *John Jones is boring.*

Qualifiers are words that limit, such as: *virtually all* (or *none*), *most, generally, usually, often, some, occasionally, seldom, rarely.* Perhaps you can add to the list. A valid syllogism can often be derived from a qualified generalization, as in:

Some English teachers are boring.
John Jones is an English teacher.
 ∴ John Jones may be boring.

Directions:
 Write "true" or "false" in the line to the left of each generalization.
For example:

__false__ a. Horses are better than ponies.

__true__ b. All men are mortal.

Nobody (well, *almost* nobody) said logic was easy!

_____ 1. Girls are smarter than boys.

_____ 2. Dogs are expensive.

_____ 3. Months have more than 27 days.

_____ 4. Snakes are poisonous.

_____ 5. Fire can be deadly.

_____ 6. Spiders often have nine legs.

_____ 7. Criminals can not be reformed.

_____ 8. Good science students do poorly in the Humanities.

_____ 9. It is usually cooler at night than during the day.

_____10. Everybody loves Disneyland.

III. Summarize

Write a summary of this lecture. It should be about ten to twelve sentences long. Use your own words, paraphrasing what the lecturer has said.

IV. Discuss

1. Videotape a TV commercial and watch it in class. In small groups, analyze its logic (or misuse of logic). Have each group explain to the class what they think are the commercial's hidden assumptions and whether or not they are valid.

2. Have each student bring a magazine or newspaper advertisement to class. Then have each group select one of the advertisements; analyze its logic (or misuse of logic), and explain your analysis to the class.

3. In small groups, create two syllogisms: one that begins with a true generalization and draws a valid conclusion, and another that begins with a false generalization. Write the two syllogisms on the board, and have the class as a whole identify which ones are valid and why.

4. Have each group choose one of the lecturer's assertions which are

listed below. Explain to the class what it means, and why you agree or disagree with it. If the group can not reach consensus, summarize each of the varied views.

a. "In a sense, the 'word' created the world."
b. "If you use 'logos' properly, you can create your own world."
c. "Only you can make yourself powerful."
d. "Only you can give an object value."

5. In small groups, create two advertisements for a product or service that you make up. One ad should be based on valid logic, and the other not. You may use words, pictures, skits – feel free to be creative. Imagine the ad in any medium you choose, such as magazines, newspapers, radio or TV. Present the two advertisements to the class. Then listen closely as the class discusses which ad is more logical and why. Explain your group's viewpoint on the ads only after the class has finished discussing them.

V. Write

1. Consider the role of emotion in the misuse of logic. Use specific examples to illustrate your opinion.

2. Have you ever observed an example of stereotyping? Have you, like most people, ever been the victim of stereotyping? In an essay, describe what happened.

3. Write an essay based on the cause/effect pattern "If p, then q." Use valid logic and appropriate qualifiers. For example, you might argue that understanding logic may help someone be a better decision maker. Support your thesis by using specific examples.

4. Topics 1 through 4 in *IV. Discuss* can be adapted and developed in writing.

Unit 13

How Food Chains Work
a Biology Lecture
by
Ann Lopez

I. Comprehend the Lecture

Watch the lecture, taking notes as conscientiously as you can. If you need more time to write, stop the tape. Listen to the lecture as many times as you wish.

Answer the following questions by referring to your notes. If necessary, watch the lecture again and add to your notes.

1. Define *ecosystems*:_____

_____

2. Give at least three examples of ecosystems: _____

_____

3. What are *components*?_____

_____

4. What do ecologists do?_____

_____

5. What happens if any part of the ecosystem is altered?

_____

6. Define *autotrophs*, and give an example: _____

_____

7. What is the pigment that green plants use to transform sunlight

energy into food?_____

8. What is the name for the process of changing sunlight into food?

_____

9. Define *heterotrophs*, and give an example: _____

_____

10. About how many people live on our planet?_____

11. What three autotrophs are they dependent on? _____

_____

12. What do *decomposers* do?_____

_____

13. Give two examples of decomposers:_____

_____

14. What does *abiotic* mean? _____

15. Give three examples of abiotic features affecting the ecosystem:

_____

_____

16. Who are the primary producers in the food chain?

_____

17. What is the shape of a diagram representing the food chain?

_____

18. How much energy is lost when one organism converts it to

another?_____

19. What is most of that "lost" energy used for?_____

_____

20. What do all organisms depend on to survive, either directly or in-

directly? _____

II. Recognize Key Points

A. Word Parts

Biology has a language of its own. Because much of that language is based on Latin, and much of English is too, learning biological terms improves your vocabulary for general English as well.

Write the meaning of each word part listed, and the meaning of the sample that uses it:

For example:
    auto- means <u>self</u>
    sample word: *automobile* means <u>self-moving</u>

1. *synthe-* means _____

    sample word: *synthetic* means _____

2. *photo-* means _____

    sample word: *photosynthesis* means_____

3. *bio-* means _____

    sample word: *biology* means_____

4. *a-* means _____

    sample word: *abiotic* means _____

5. *-troph* means _____

    sample word: *atrophy* means_____

6. *hetero-* means _____

    sample word: *heterogeneous* means_____

7. *homo-* means _____

    sample word: *homogeneous* means_____

B. Outline

Ann Lopez presents a highly organized lecture. The advantage of outlining as you take notes is that you are organizing ideas and understanding relationships as they're explained.

If you can't manage to outline at the same time you're taking notes, outlining them later can be a good review.

Directions: Fill in the blanks to complete these outlined notes taken during the lecture. Notice the use of abbreviations and symbols.

How Food Chains Work
Friday, October 22

I.   Ecosystems = giant assemblages of _____

_____ all interacting together

Ex. = redwood forest, trop. rain forest, arctic tundra

II. Components = _____

   A.   Ecologists study their _____ = what

   ties them together

   B.   _____ = wholes

   C.   If any part altered, the _____ changes,

   usually declining

III. Autotrophs

   A.   Self-feeders (auto = _____, troph = _____)

   B.   _____ plants do this thanks to

   _____ = pigment that –> radiant sunlight

   energy into _____

   C.   Leaves make _____

   D.   All organisms on our planet , indirectly or directly, depend on

   this process = photosynthesis (photo = _____,

   synthesis = _____)

E. Sunlight –> food

IV. Heterotrophs

   A. Mixed-feeders (hetero = _____)

   B. All animals and fungi, including _____

   C. 6 billion people depend on_____

V. Decomposers

   A. Take _____& put

     their nutrients back into the system

   B. Bacteria & fungi

   C. Provide_____ with what they need

VI. Abiotic factors

   A. Nonliving organisms (a = _____,

     bio =_____)

   B. Temp., humidity, amt. sunlight, precipt., type of soil

VII. Food chains

   A. Autotrophs = _____ producers

   B. Pyramid shaped because when an organism is converted, it

     loses_____ of its energy.

   C. Most of our energy goes into_____

D. Ex. cow eats 10 lbs of grass, gains only _____ pound

of weight

E. We eat the cow. A lot of grass —> one portion of _____

on a dinner plate.

III. Summarize

Write a summary of this lecture. It should be about ten to twelve sentences long. Use your own words, paraphrasing what the lecturer has said.

IV. Discuss

1. A quiz would be likely to ask students to define the four major components in an ecosystem and their functions. In small groups, discuss the best way to learn this information so that you could supply it on a quiz without using your notes. Have each group share its study suggestions with the class as a whole.

2. College students are expected to memorize terms, but they also need to understand processes and concepts, and be able to apply them. Have each student bring an item or a picture to class and explain where and how it fits in a food chain.

3. A local television station has invited your class, which is a well-known environmental club, to present a program about dangers to the food chain that would result from the destruction of a large redwood forest (or the tropical rain forest, or any ecosystem you choose). The class will design the show, being sure that each student has a part in the production. If you wish, some class members can choose not to be in the environmental club, and instead play the role of forest developers or executives in a logging company, arguing an alternative point of view. Videotape your program.
When you view the videotape, assess the logic of the arguments.

4. Imagine this scenario:

The city owns twenty-five acres of land now used to grow wheat. Bread made from the wheat is distributed to needy people. Developer Sara Smith has offered to buy the land so she can build a shopping mall on it. James Johnson wants to buy the land to start a ranch for raising beef cattle. Should the land be sold to either of these people?

Organize a debate. The debate leader will play the part of the mayor who will make the final decision. However, that decision will not be made unilaterally. The mayor has organized a public meeting in which Sara Smith and her staff will discuss their plans; also present to defend their plan will be James Johnson and his staff. The public will listen and voice their opinions to the mayor as well.

V. Write

1. Topics 2, 3 and 4 in *IV. Discuss* can be developed in writing.

2. Write a paragraph explaining why the food chain is represented by a pyramid.

3. Imagine that you have grown corn in your garden. In a paragraph, explain where corn fits in a typical food chain.

4. Choose your own topic relating to food chains that you would like to learn more about. Formulate a precise question that your research will answer.

Unit 14

Aging
a Health Lecture
by
Priscilla Brown

I. Comprehend the Lecture

Watch the lecture, taking notes as conscientiously as you can. If you need more time to write, stop the tape. Listen to the lecture as many times as you wish.

Answer the following questions by referring to your notes. If necessary, watch the lecture again and add to your notes.

1. Define *aging*: _____

_____

2. What are two characteristics normally associated with aged people?

_____

3. Name the first theory of aging that Dr. Brown describes:

_____

4. In explaining the theory, what does she compare the human body

to? _____

5. What is the second theory? _____

6. Briefly explain this theory, and give at least two examples of its

occurrence:_____

_____

_____

_____

7. What is the third theory? _____

8. Briefly explain this theory:_____

_____

9. Where do newborn babies get their antibodies?

_____

10. At what age do babies start manufacturing their own?

_____

11. (yes, no) Does the lecturer say one of these theories is the most

convincing? _____

12. Do these theories oppose each other, or do they overlap?

_____

13. Name two behaviors that contribute to people's ill health:

_____

14. What old saying does the lecturer refer to? _____

_____

15. At what age does the normal person's health peak? _____

16. At what age does a person become a "senior citizen"? _____

17. What is one reason why the cancer risk may be much higher for an

older person than a younger one?_____

_____

II. Respond to the lecture

A. Theories

The health sciences investigate many theories. A theory is an idea that seems to explain many specific phenomena, but it is not proven; in other words, a theory is a generalization that is not known to hold true for all cases. When a theory does apply in all cases, scientists call it a "law."

For example, pick up an object that is not breakable, and then let go of it. It fell, didn't it?   It is subject to the law of gravity. As long as we stay within the earth's atmosphere (notice this qualifier), gravity will make all things move downward.

B. Similes

Dr. Brown compares the human body to a clock. She uses a *simile*, saying that in the wear and tear theory, the body is "like a clock." A *simile* says that one thing is *like* another; in contrast, a metaphor says that one thing *is* another. The second theory suggests that the human body is in fact a clock that changes according to a pre-programmed, timed calendar.

Similes and metaphors are typically studied within the realm of literature, yet Dr. Brown, a physician, has used them in her lecture. Comparisons help to clarify new information, especially if it is abstract or unfamiliar. Notice how disciplines overlap. Synthesizing ideas from several perspectives is a hallmark of good scholarship.

Directions: In a complete sentence, create a simile or metaphor that describes each of these concepts.

For example:

a freeway: The freeway interchange is like a can of worms.
a transcript: The graduate's transcript is the key that opens the door of employment opportunity.

1. wallet: _____

_____

2. youth: _____

_____

3. corn: _____

_____

4. cup of coffee: _____

_____

5. grandma: _____

_____

6. English: _____

_____

III. Summarize

Write a summary of this lecture. It should be about ten to twelve sentences long. Use your own words, paraphrasing what the lecturer has said.

IV. Discuss

1. Aging is a process that all people undergo, but different cultures have different attitudes about it. Have one group of students summarize the dominant American cultural attitudes toward aging. Have other groups describe attitudes toward aging held by people of other eras, cultures or American subcultures. Conduct any needed research, and have each group report their findings to the class.

2. Get into small groups. The task of each group is to construct a theory relating to health, and a way to test it. Your theory may be humorous or serious, having to do with people in your small group, your families, animals, etc. Conduct your tests, compile and interpet the results, and be prepared to explain your entire process to the class.

V. Write

1. In a paragraph, explain why Dr. Brown says she'll explain three "theories," not three "laws."

2. Describe in detail an old person you know, and explain how that person's health reflects any or all of the theories of aging.

3. Write an essay explaining what you hope to accomplish by the time you reach old age.

4. Write an essay about specific ways people's behavior can affect their health.

5. Explain the saying, "Youth is wasted on the young." Do you agree?

6. Has your attitude toward aging changed as you have gotten older? If so, write an essay describing the different attitudes you have had. If not, explain the attitude you have consistently held.

7. If you could have an operation that would prevent your body from aging any more, would you have it? Explain why or why not.

8. Research done for the first topic in *IV. Discuss* can be presented in written papers.

If your instructor wants you to write a research paper on this topic, review the guidelines on conducting research in Unit 10.

Unit 15

Origins of Jazz
a Music Lecture
by
Joe Weed

I. Comprehend the Lecture

Watch the lecture, taking notes as conscientiously as you can. If you need more time to write, stop the tape. Listen to the lecture as many times as you wish.

Answer the following questions by referring to your notes. If necessary, watch the lecture again and add to your notes.

1. List four important elements of jazz: _____

_____

2. What does *improvisation* mean? _____

_____

3. Rhythm is fundamental to jazz because the music was often played

so people could _____.

4. Whereas classical music is the composer's art, jazz is the

_____ art.

5. In what continent was the birth site of jazz? _____

6. Where did Africans bring their music?_____

7. In what country has jazz reached its fruition?_____

8. Did jazz originate as a music primarily of instruments or the human

voice?_____

9. In Africa, what were the two main functions of music?

_____

10. White slave masters tried to strip away the slaves' native cultures,

but they did not succeed in removing their _____.

11. When slaves worked in the fields, what rhythmic call and response

developed?_____

12. What is the name for the religious music the slaves sang with the

approval of their masters?_____

13. What is the name for the 19th Century music whose lyrics were
about daily concerns, families, romance and problems?

_____

14. What southern American city was the center of early forms of jazz?

_____

15. What is the name for early jazz usually played on tuba, trombone,

clarinet and banjo? _____

16. Who is the most famous musician from the New Orleans era?

_____

17. After World War I, what northern city became the new center of

jazz? _____

18. As jazz grew more sophisticated, the banjo used for rhythm was

replaced by the _____

19. The tuba was replaced by the string _____.

20. Name the element of classical music that some educated jazz

musicians added to their music:_____

II. Respond to the Lecture

When he was asked to define jazz, Louis Armstrong said that if people had to ask, they would never know. The way to know, of course, is to listen to it.

To help you find examples of the music described in this lecture, here are some names of musicians whose recordings are readily available.

blues: Lightnin' Hopkins, Mississippi John Hurt, Robert Johnson, Albert King, B.B. King, Sonny Terry and Brownie McGee

Dixieland: Louis Armstrong, King Oliver, Kid Ory

early Chicago jazz: Bix Beiderbecke, Bunny Berigan, Earl "Father" Hines, Gene Krupa, Muggsy Spanier

III. Prepare for a Test

In explaining the development of early jazz, Joe Weed follows chronological order. A typical essay question based on this lecture might be:

Trace the development of early jazz from its origins to its manifestation in Chicago.

To handle this topic, first you must follow the directions: "Trace."

This means you should list key events in order. Transition words that might be useful to link the events smoothly include:

then, after that, later on, eventually, soon, next

Review your notes, and determine which events you would list in answering this question.

IV. Summarize

Write a summary of this lecture. It should be about ten to twelve sentences long. Use your own words, paraphrasing what the lecturer has said.

V. Discuss

1. Jazz originated as an African-American folk music. Research the music of another American subculture, showing how its development relates to the life style of its creators. Possibilities include but are not limited to:

- Cajun music of southern Louisiana
- Hillbilly music of the Appalachian Mountains
- Tex-Mex music from the border of Texas and Mexico
- Western Swing from Texas and Oklahoma

Organize your research in small groups, and present your findings in a panel to the whole class.

2. The professor describes the origins of jazz. Research one of the later eras of jazz development, such as Big Band, bebop, modern jazz and post-modern jazz. Organize your research in small groups, and present your findings in a panel to the whole class.

VI. Write

1. Joe Weed gives a general overview of the development of early jazz. Write a paper on one aspect of the history of jazz which you research in

depth. You might focus on a particular era, type of music, place where the music was played, etc.

2. Research and write about the life of any American musician, past or present.

3. Attend a concert and write a review of it. Imagine that you are writing for a mainstream American newspaper.

4. Survey your lecture notes looking for opinions that could be defended in an essay. Predict an essay question that the lecturer might include on a test, and write an answer to it.

5. Both of the topics in *V. Discuss* can be developed in research papers.